Gilead's Goblinz™

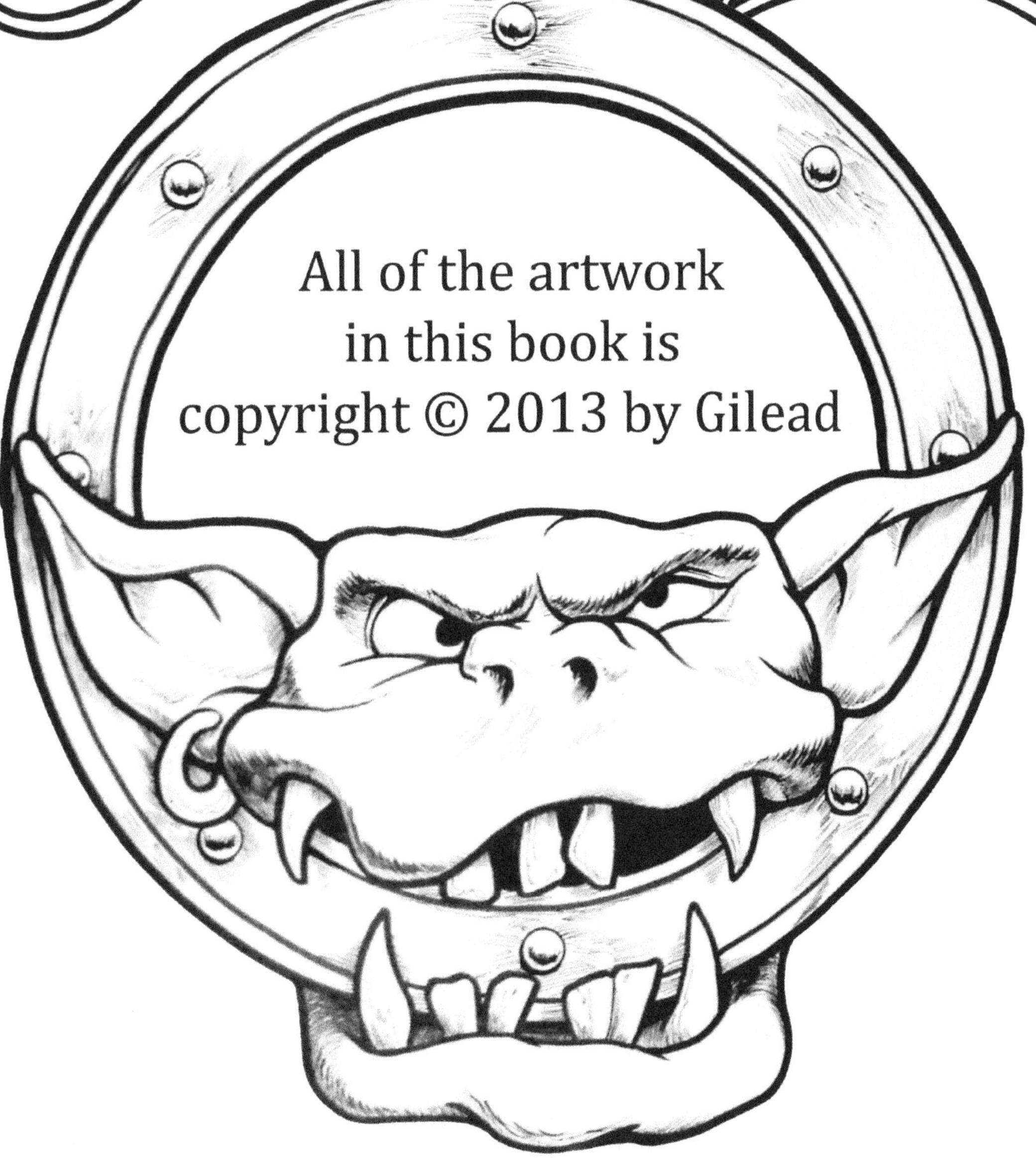

Made in U.S.A.

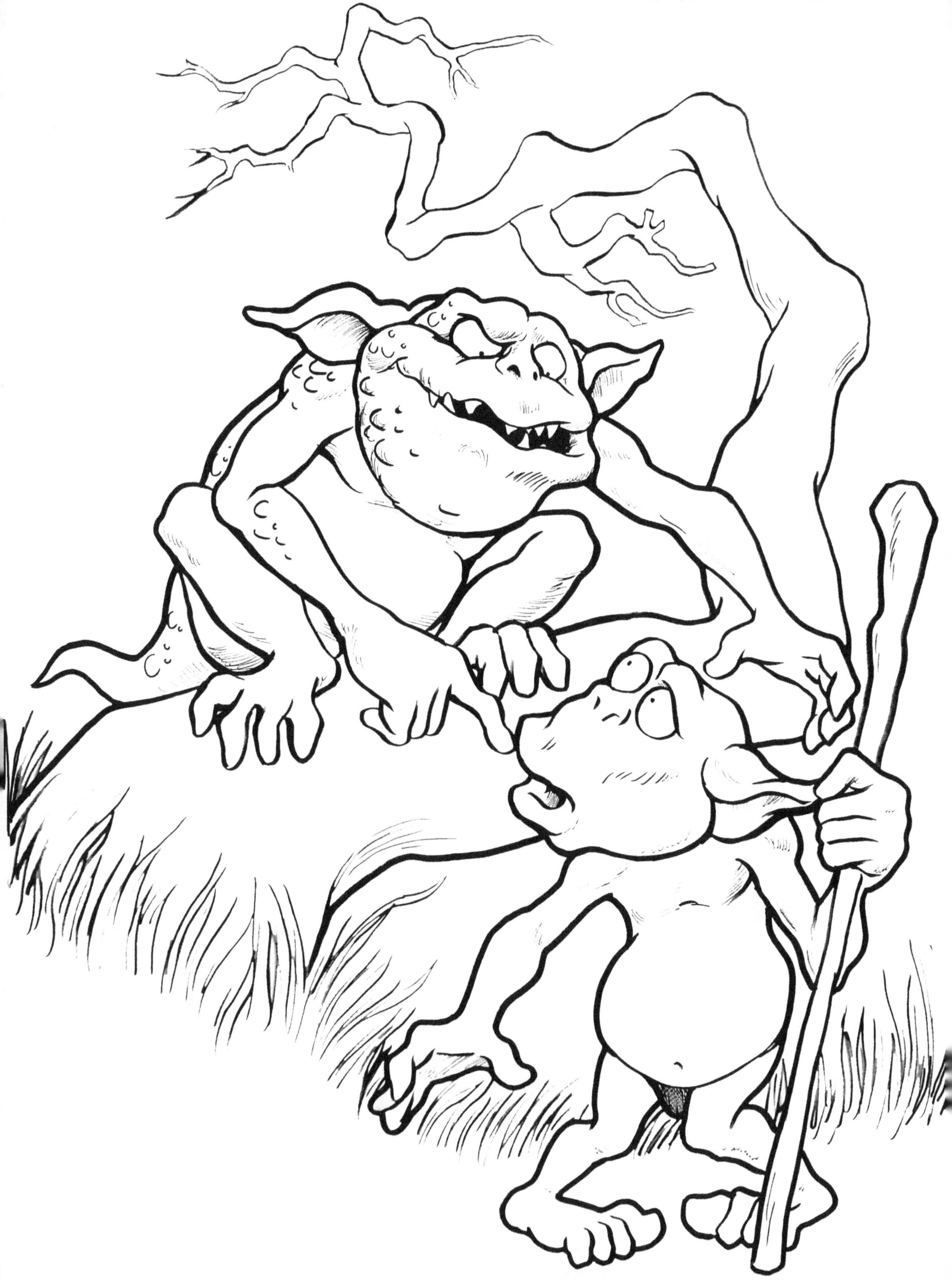

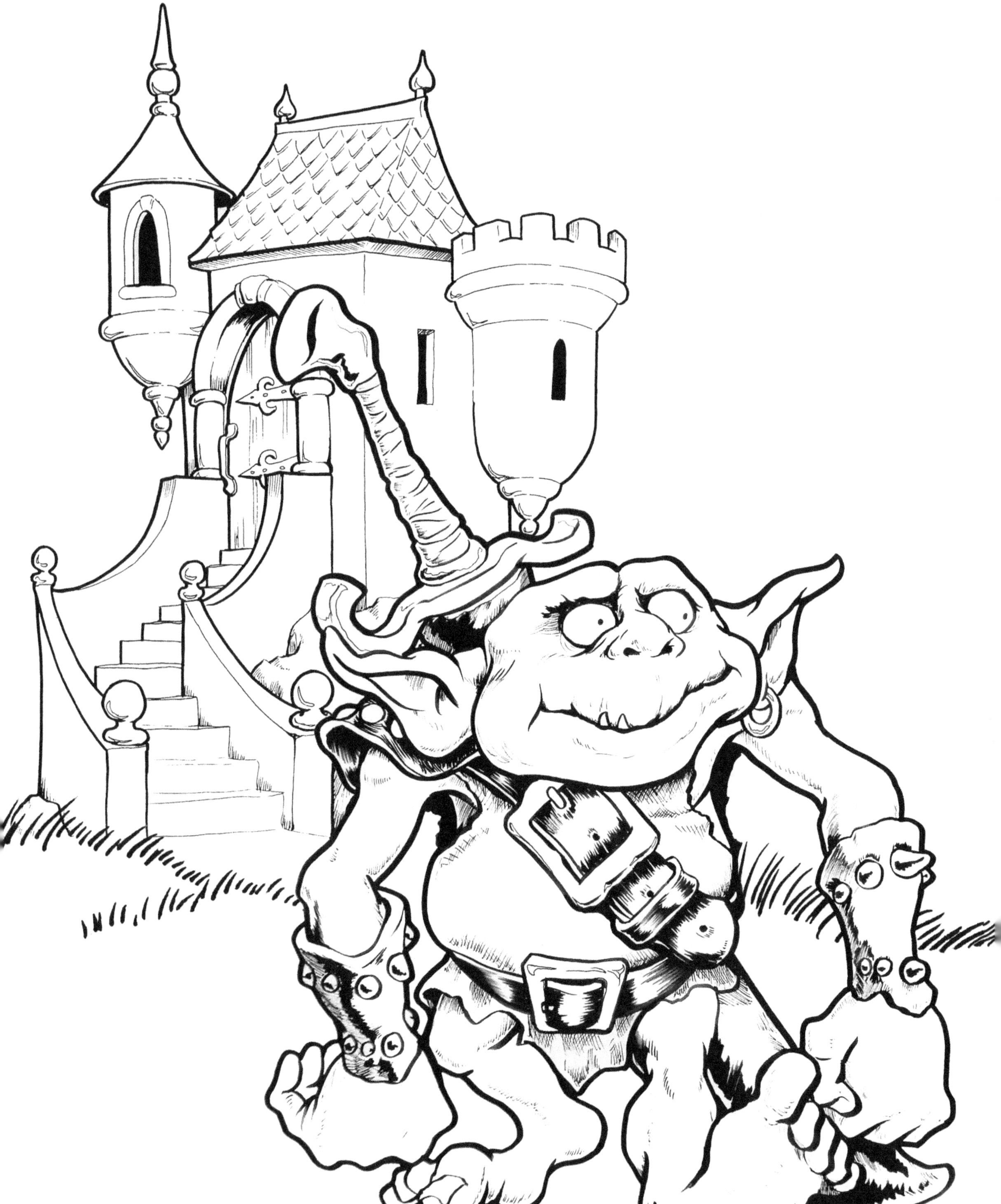

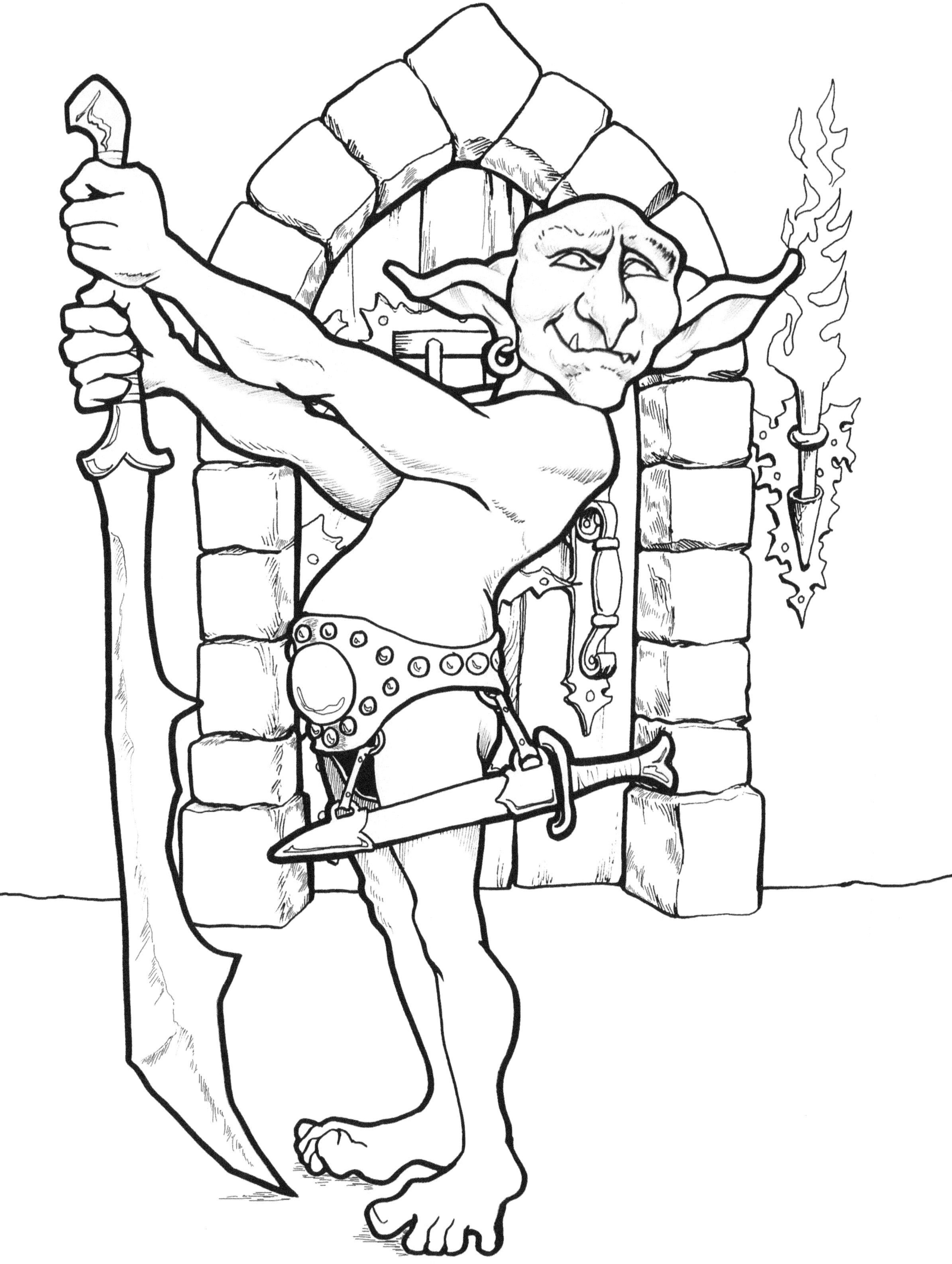

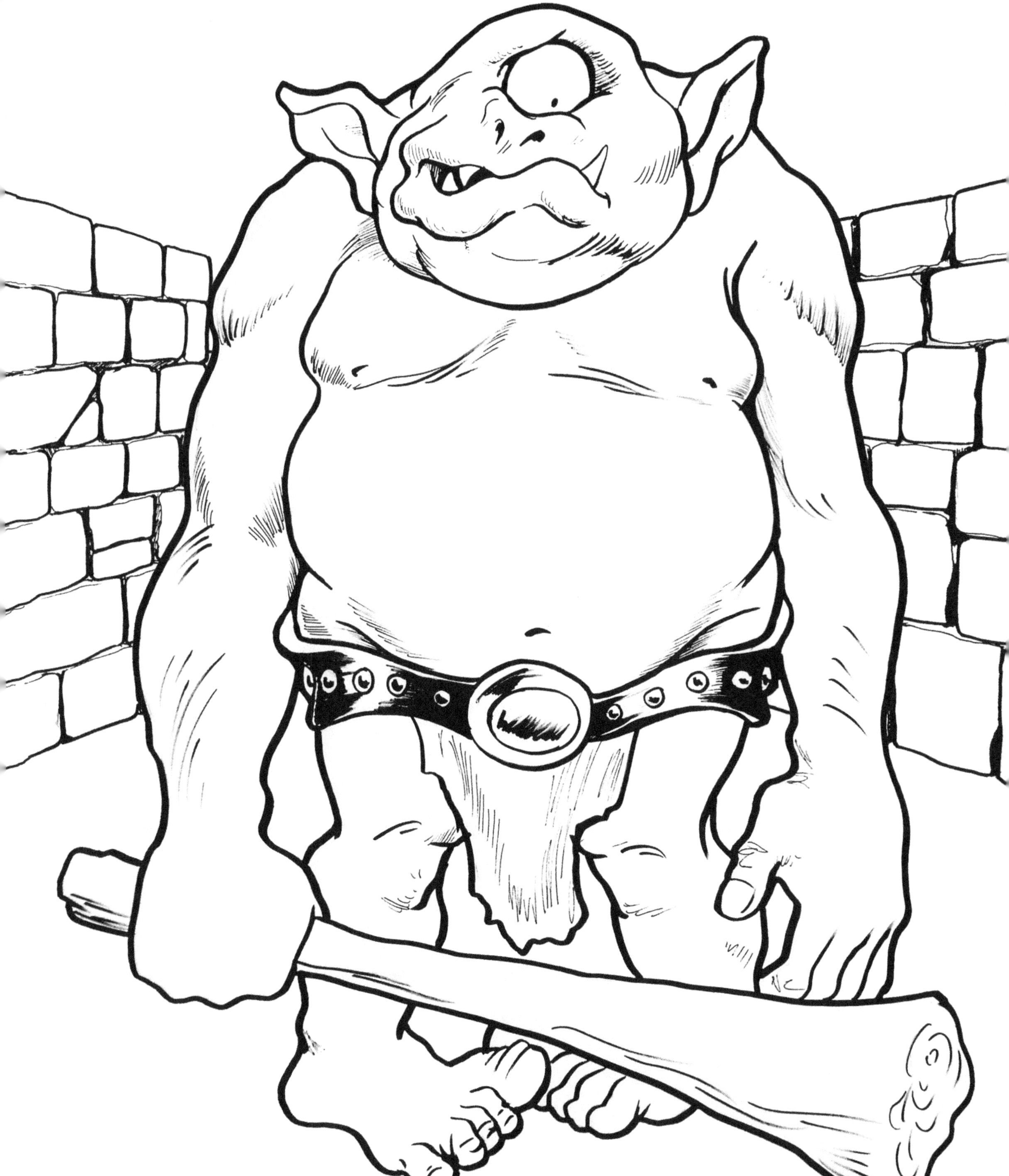

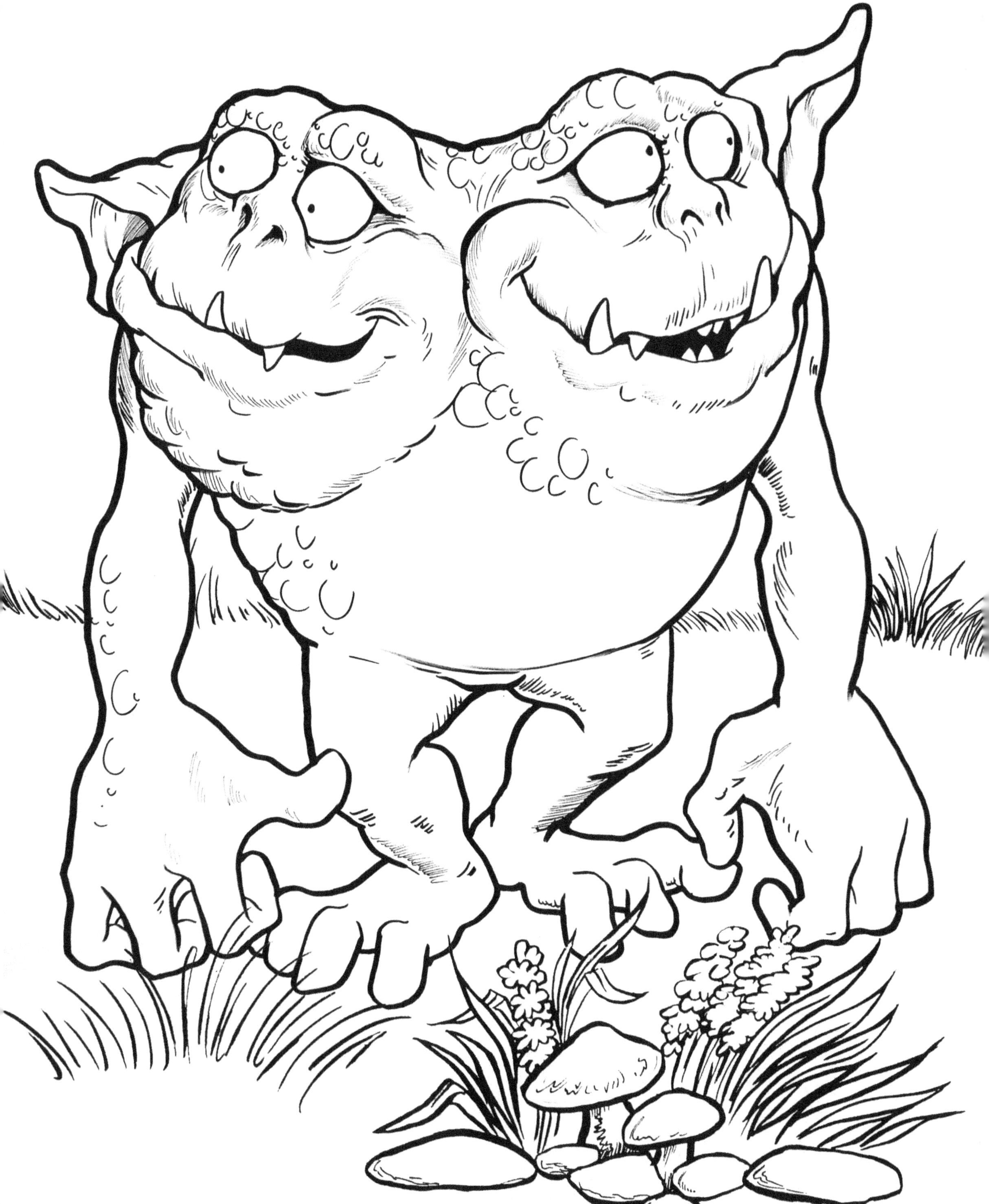

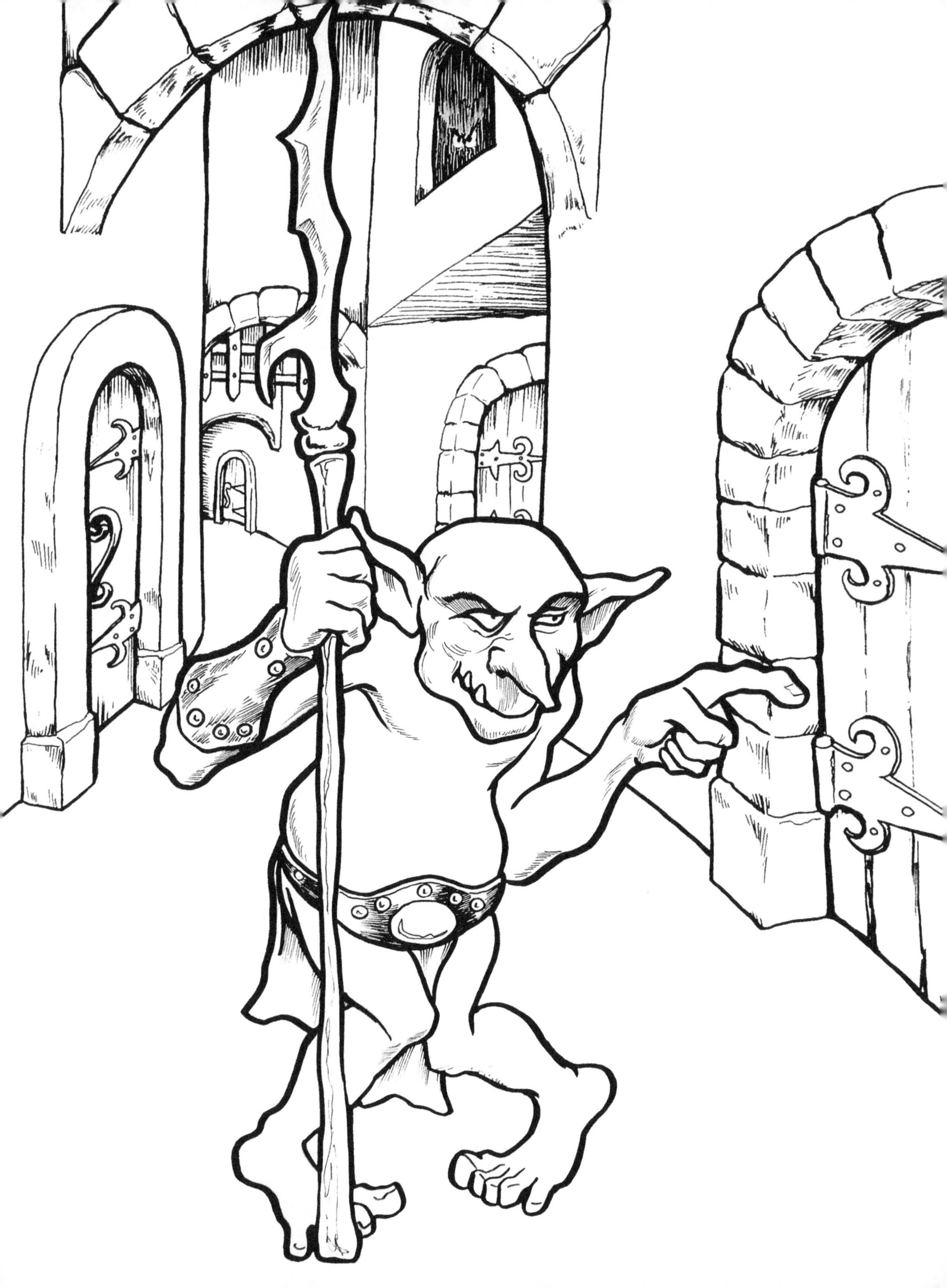

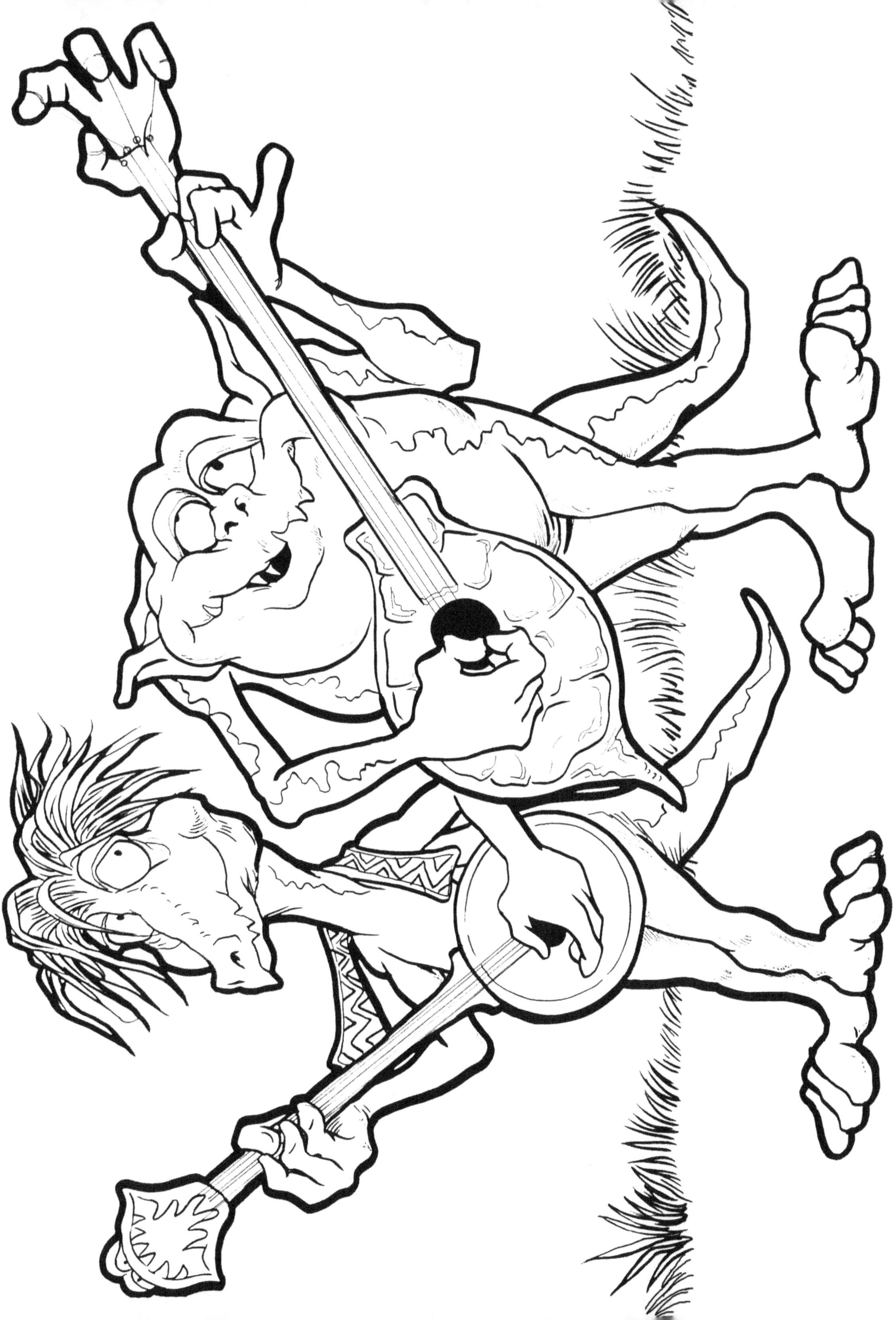

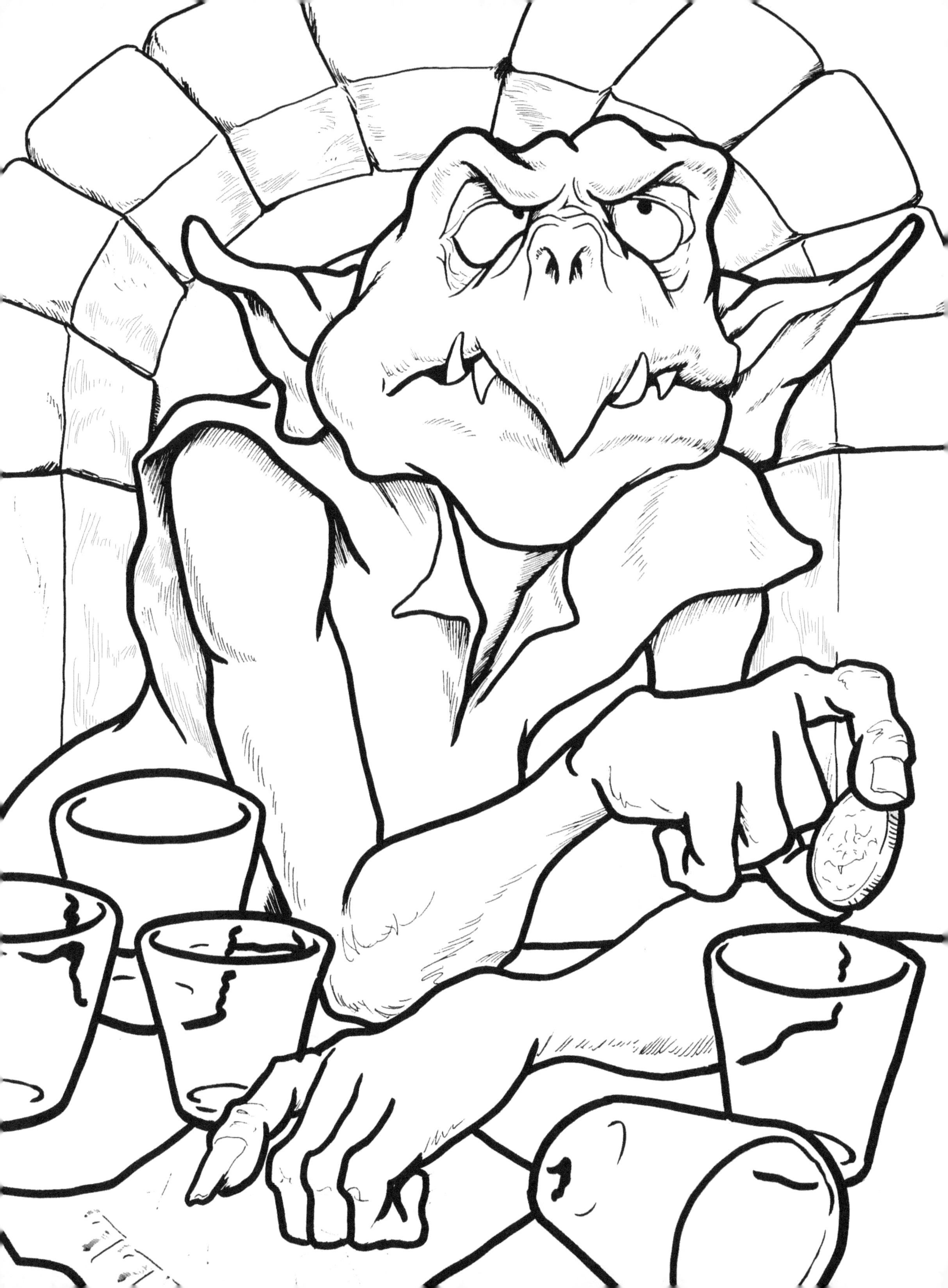

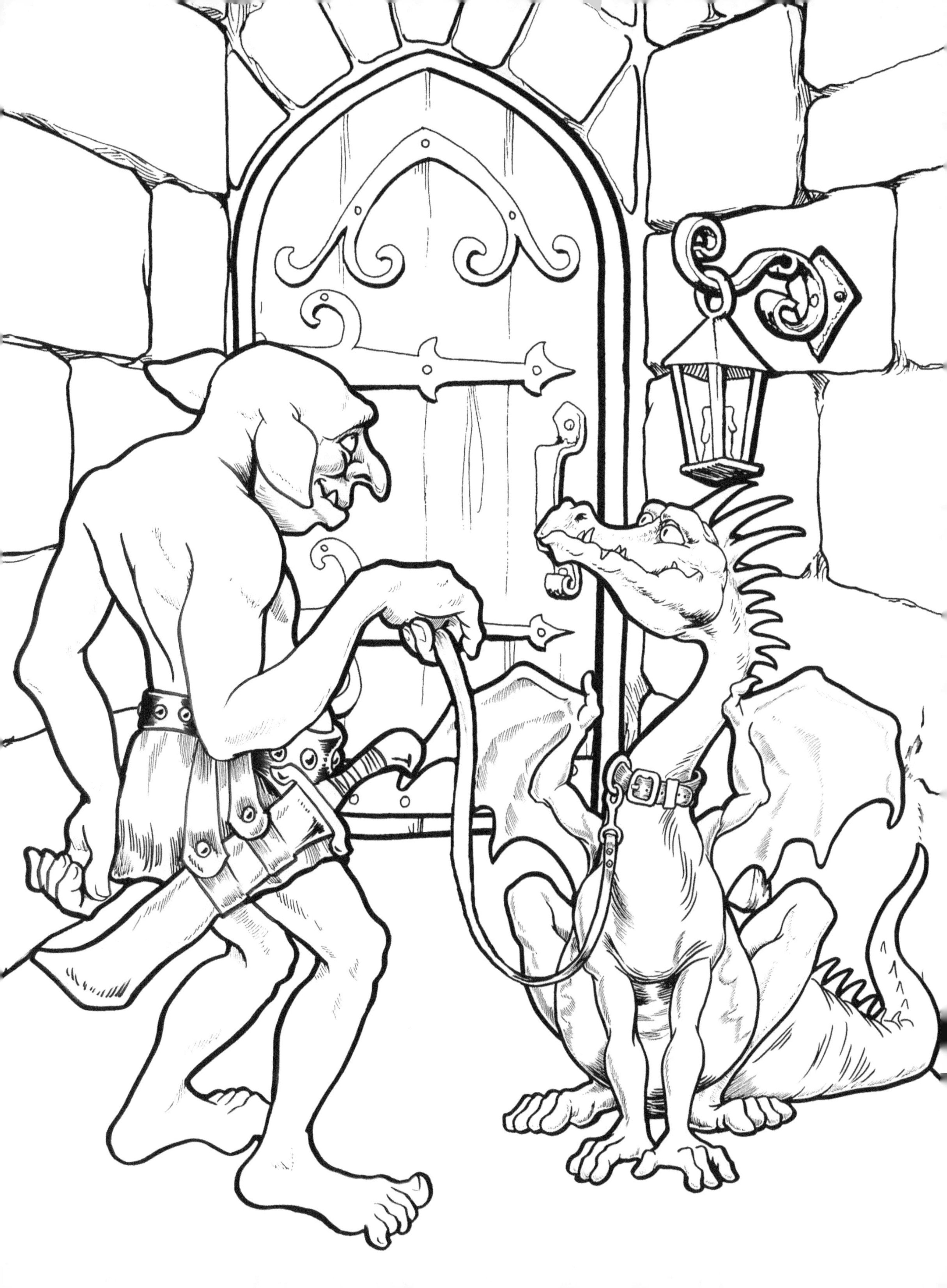

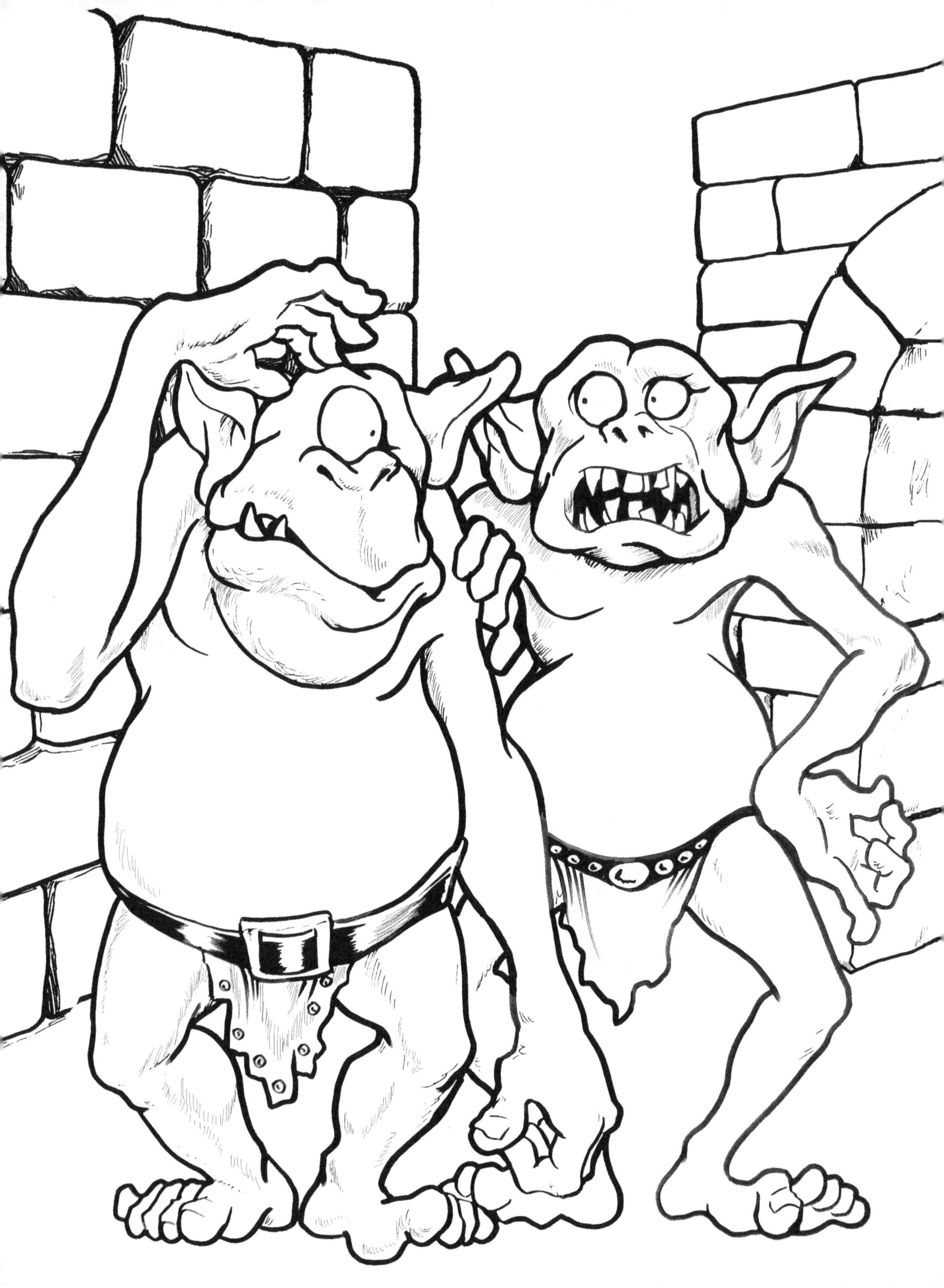

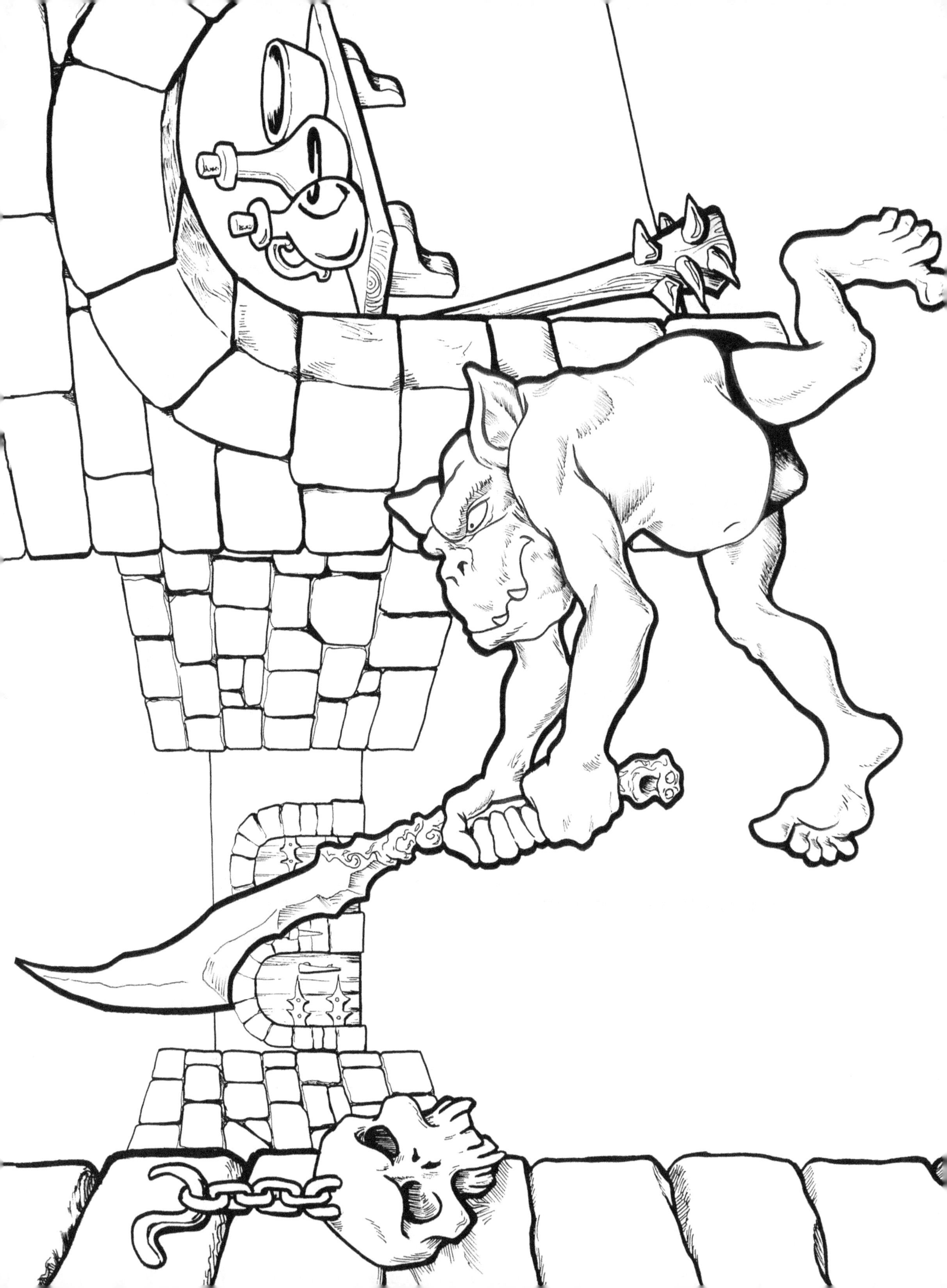

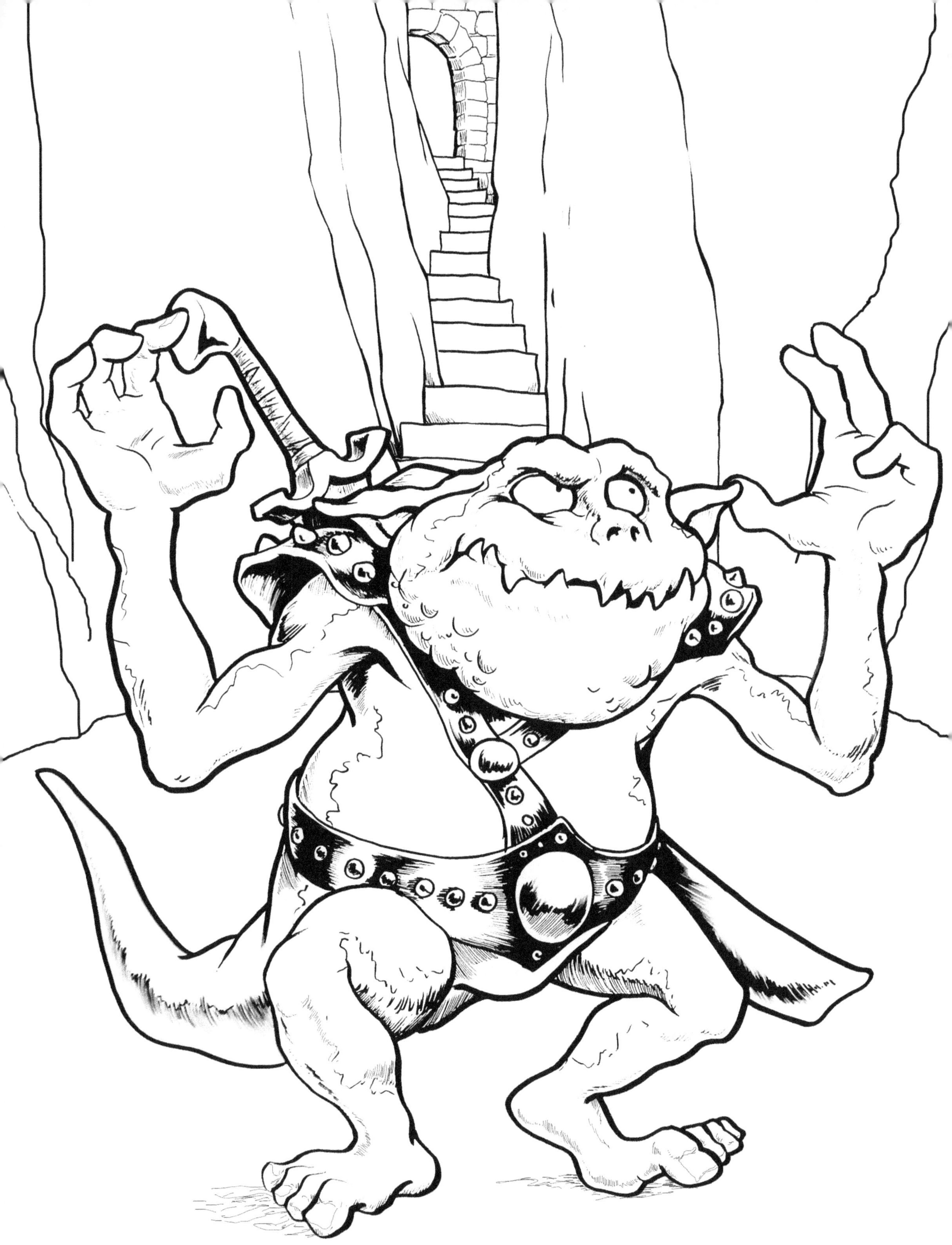

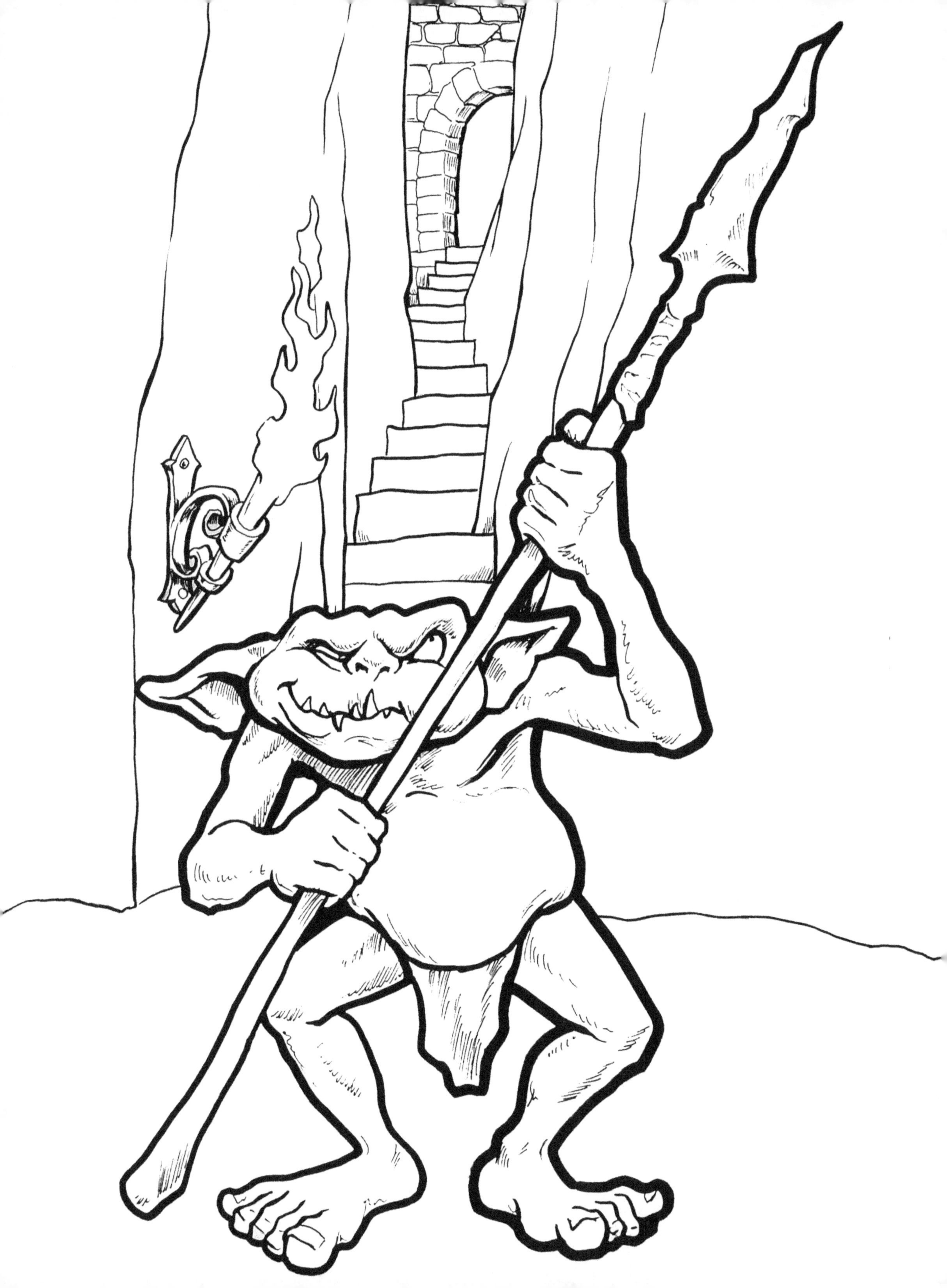

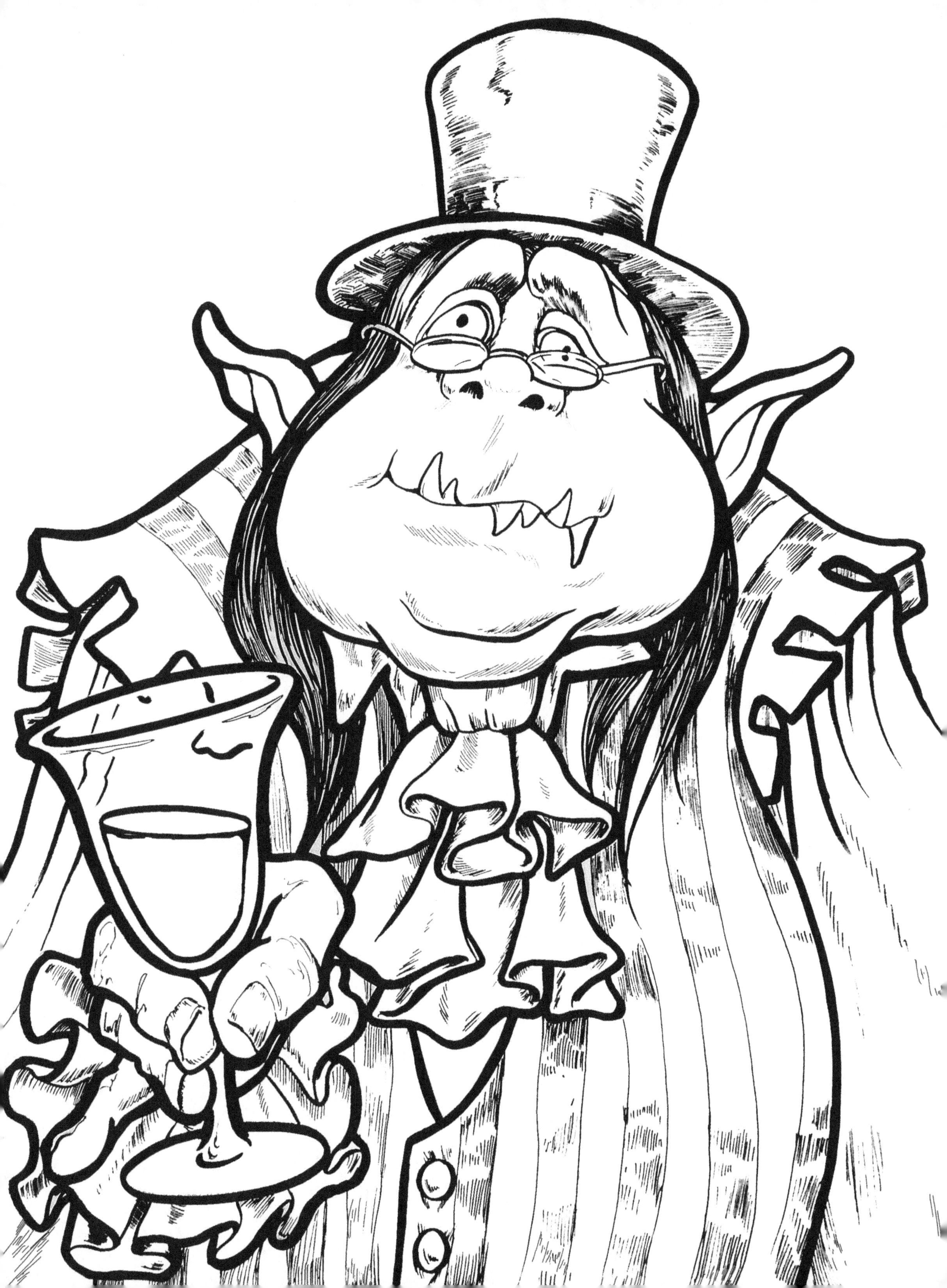

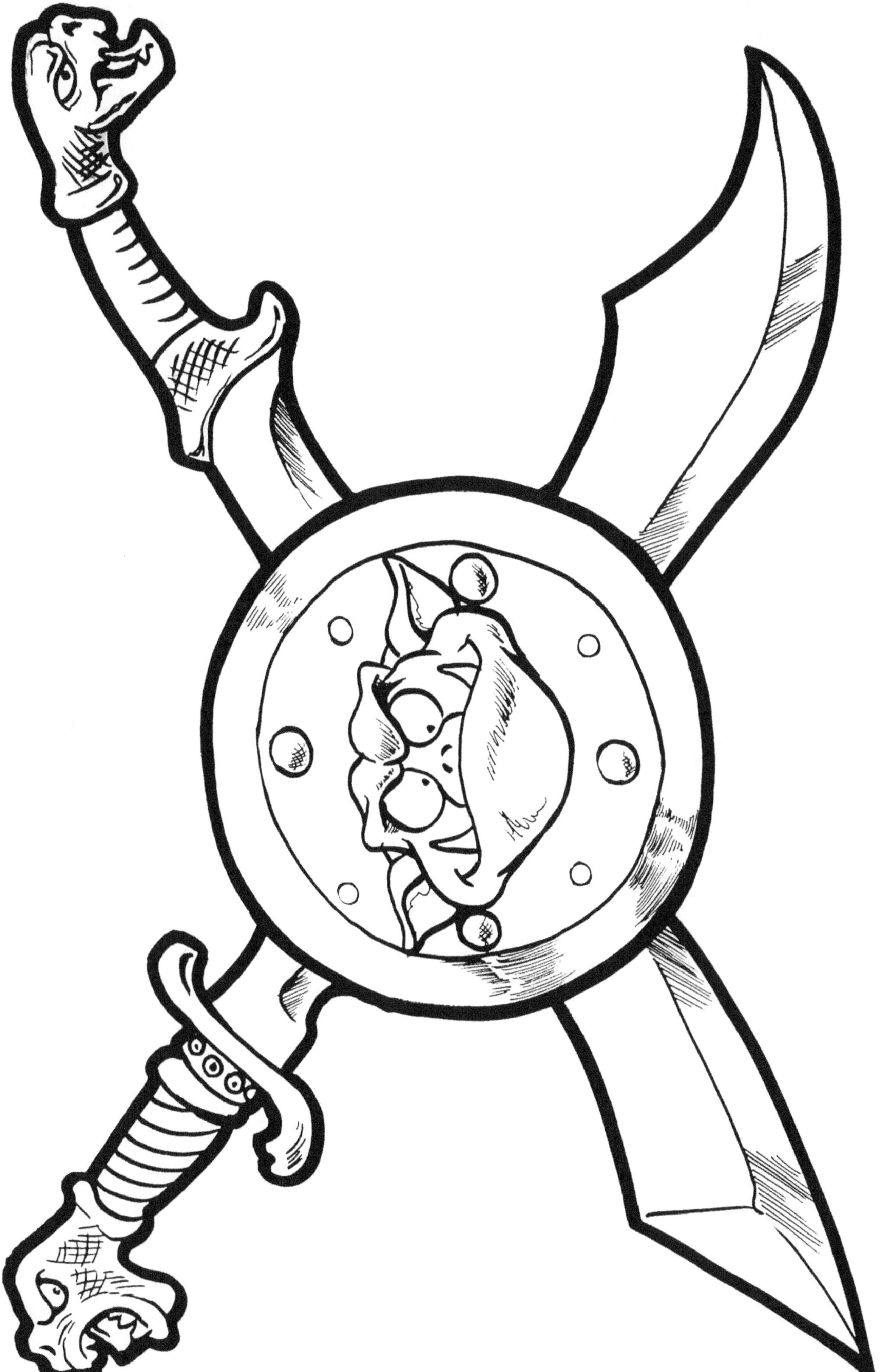

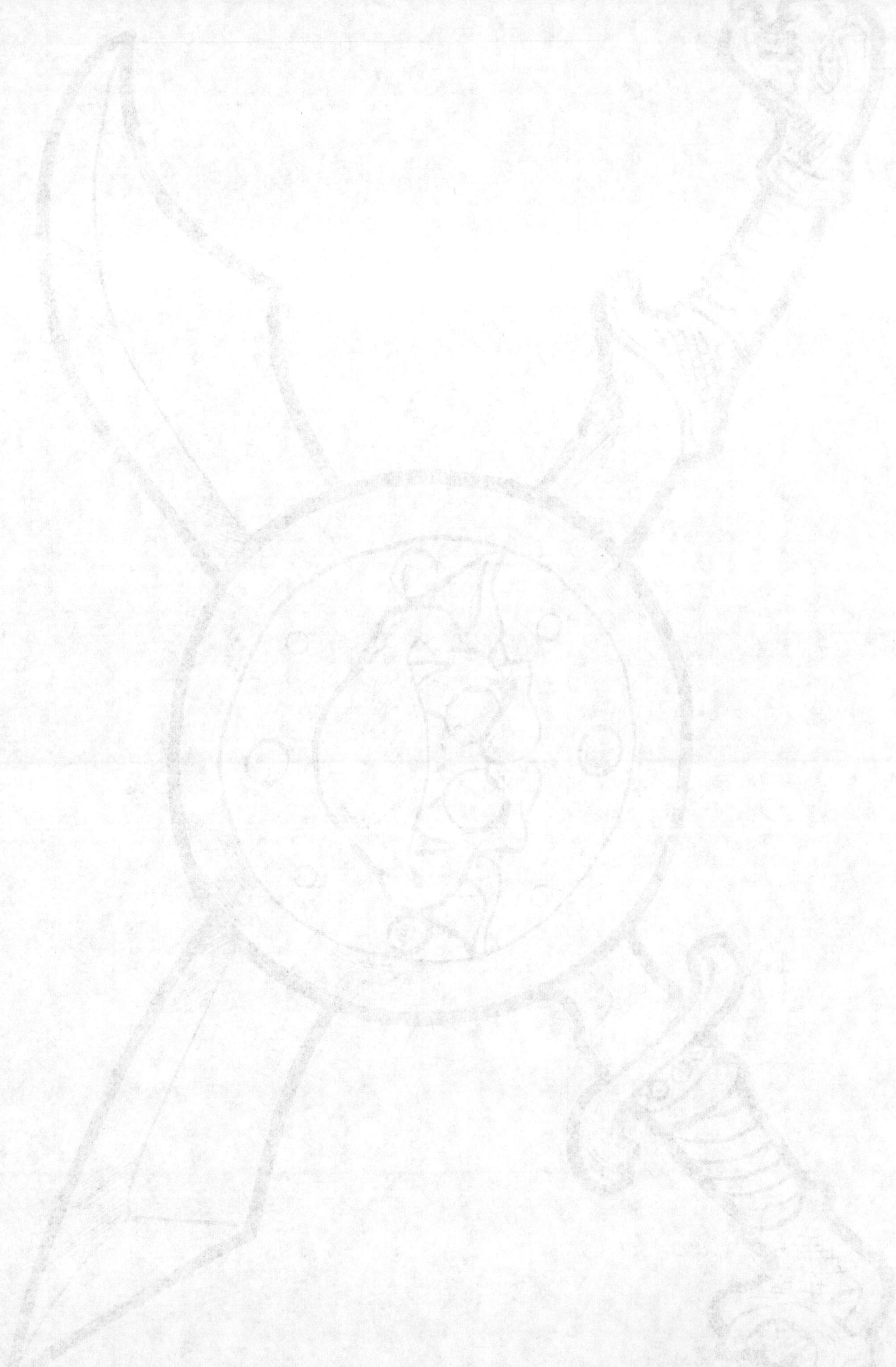

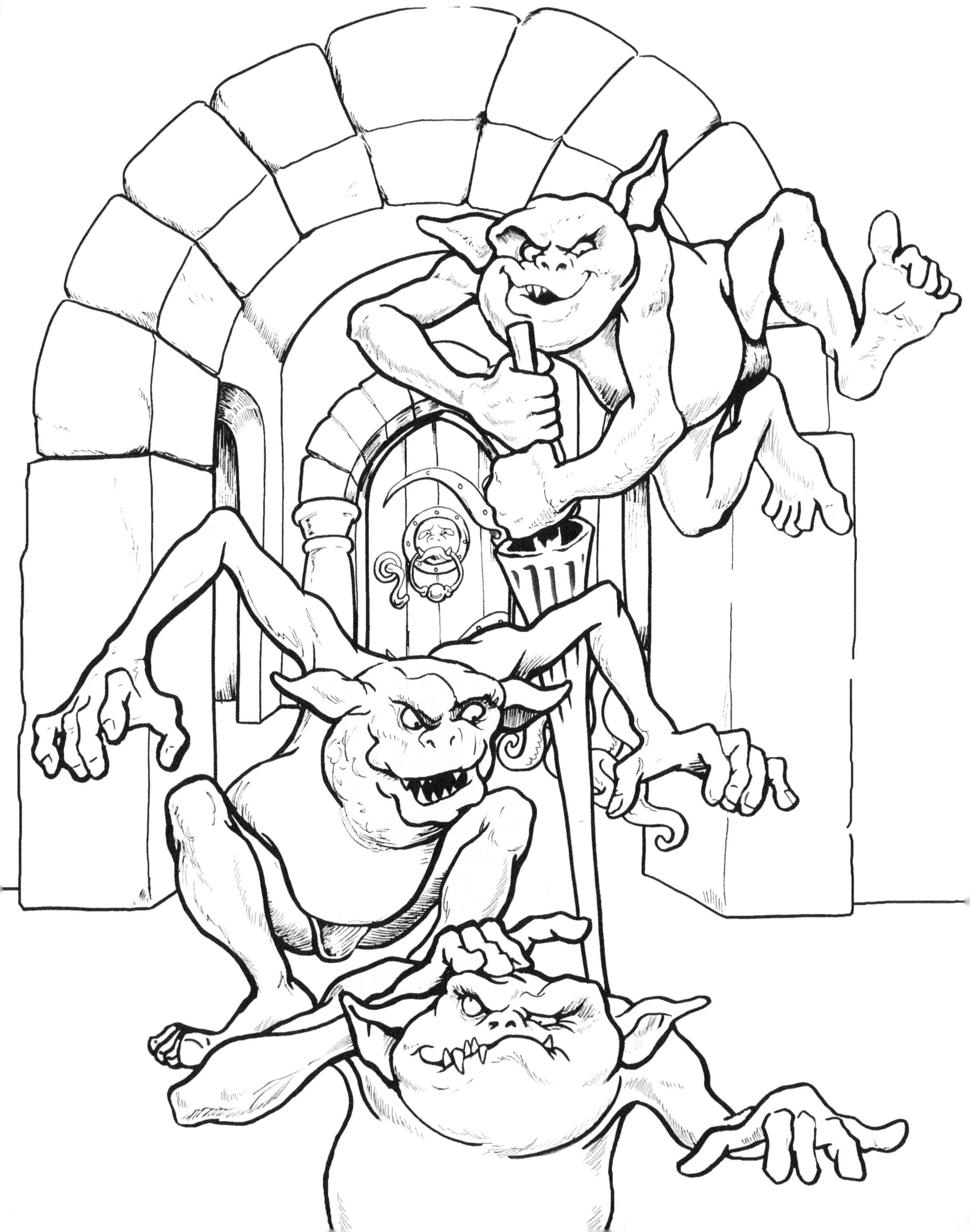

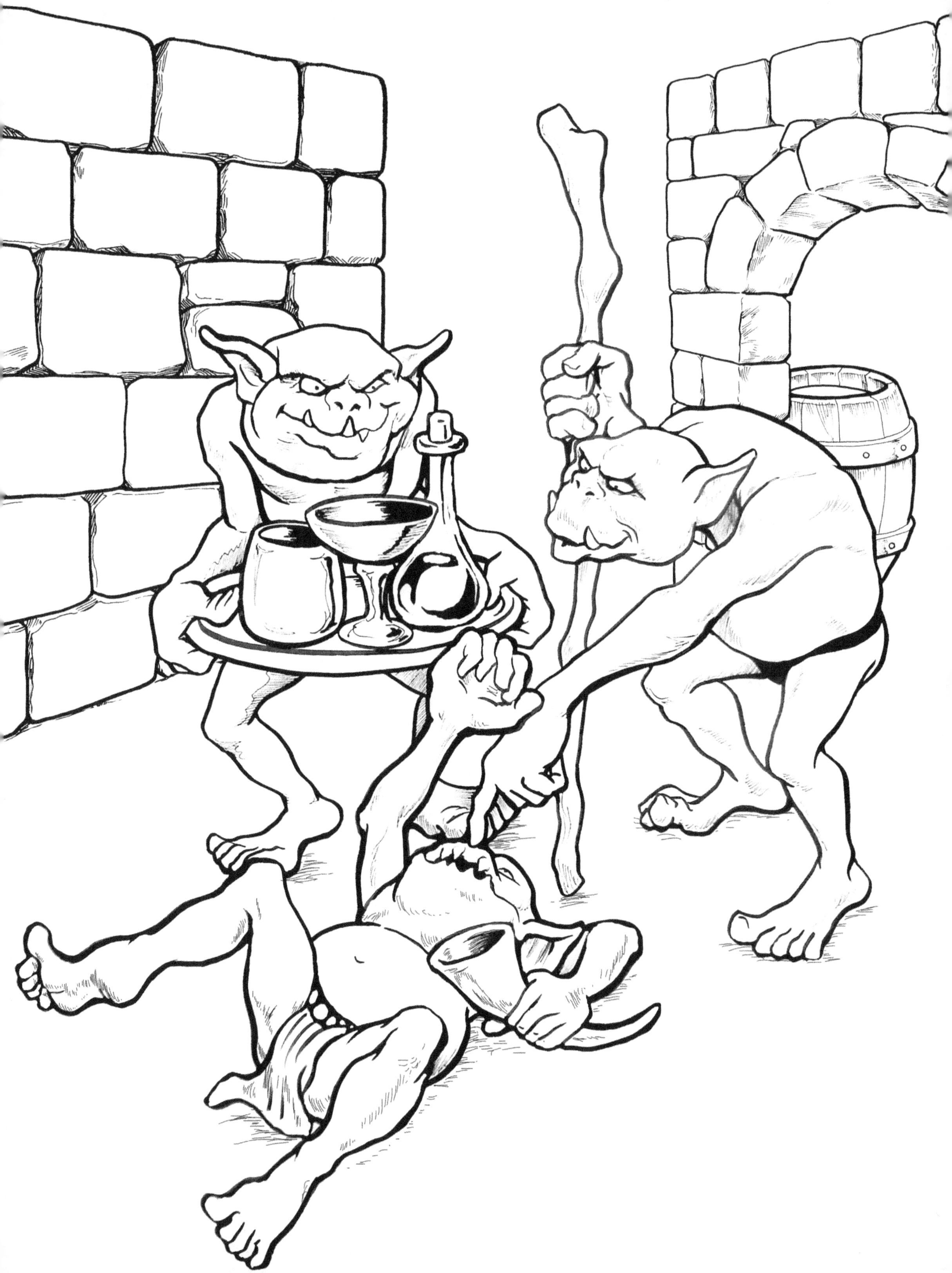

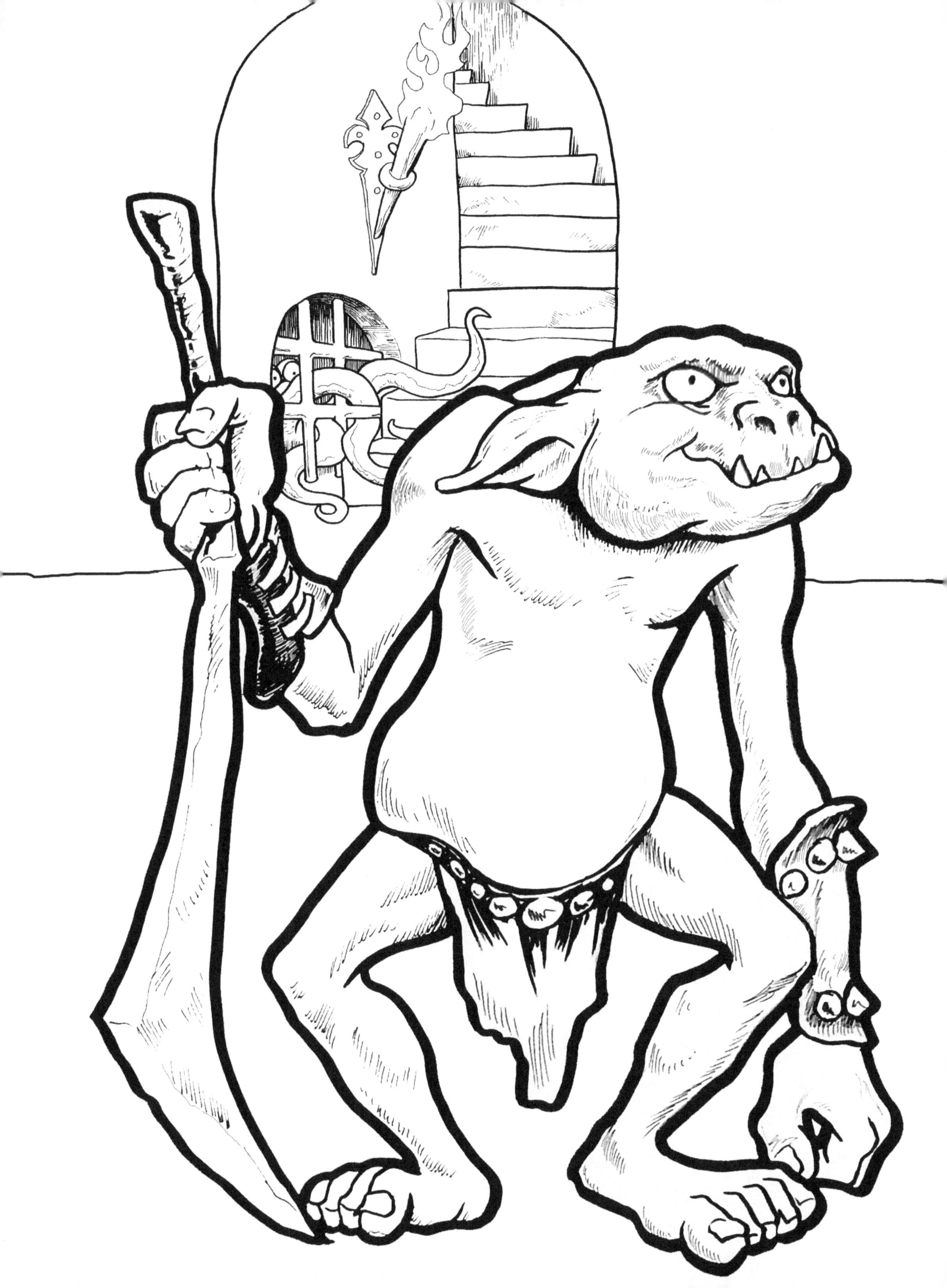

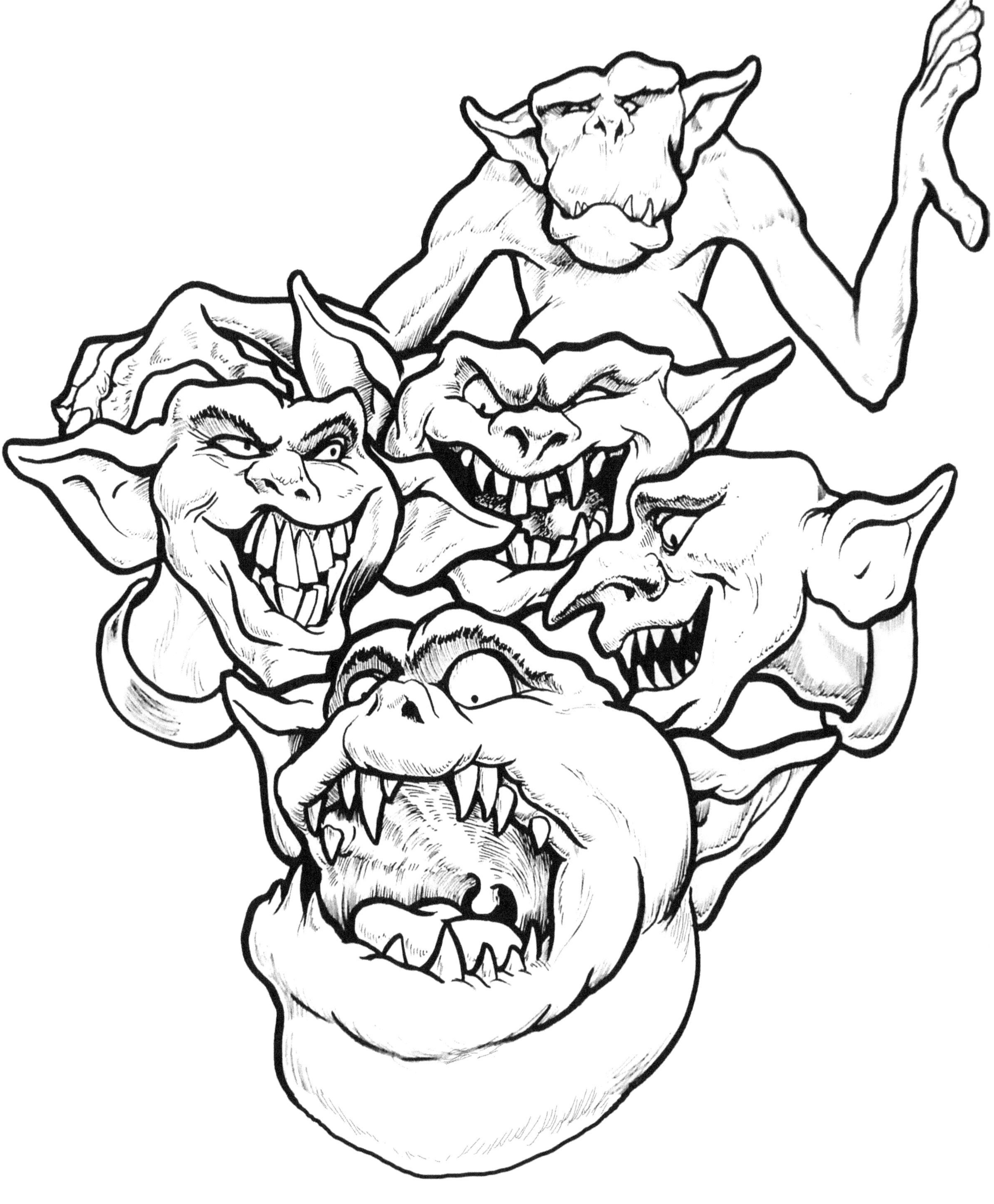

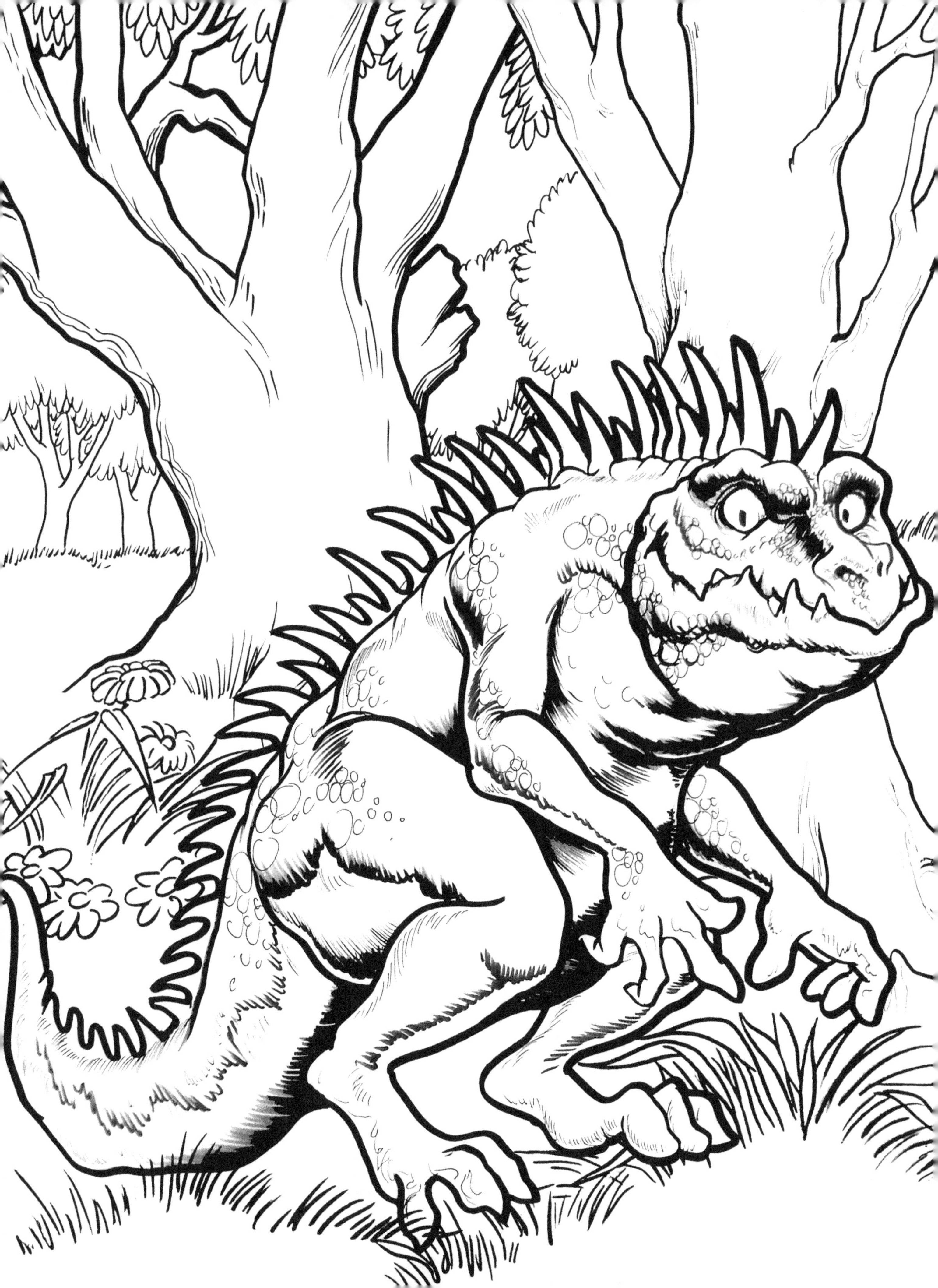

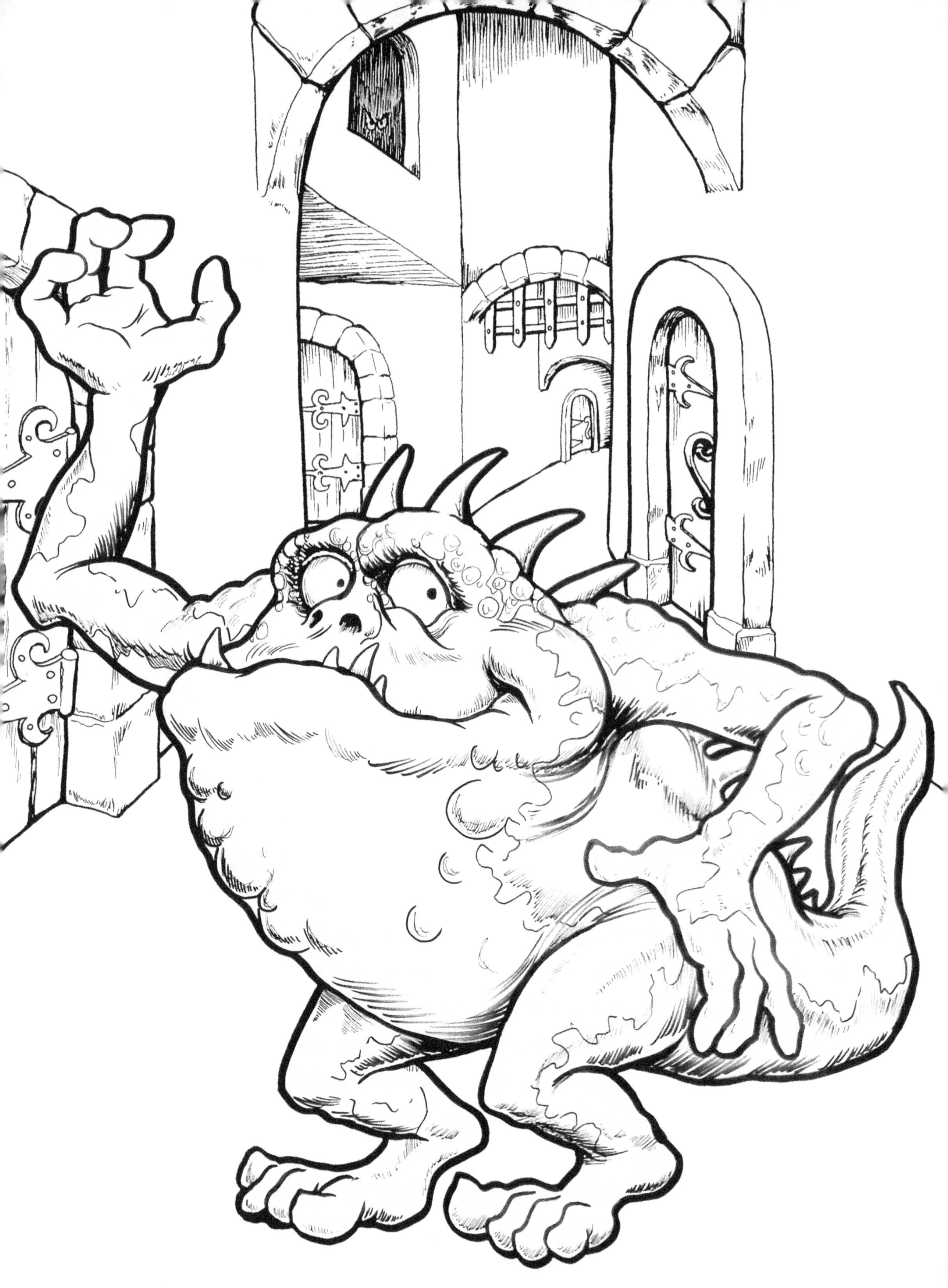

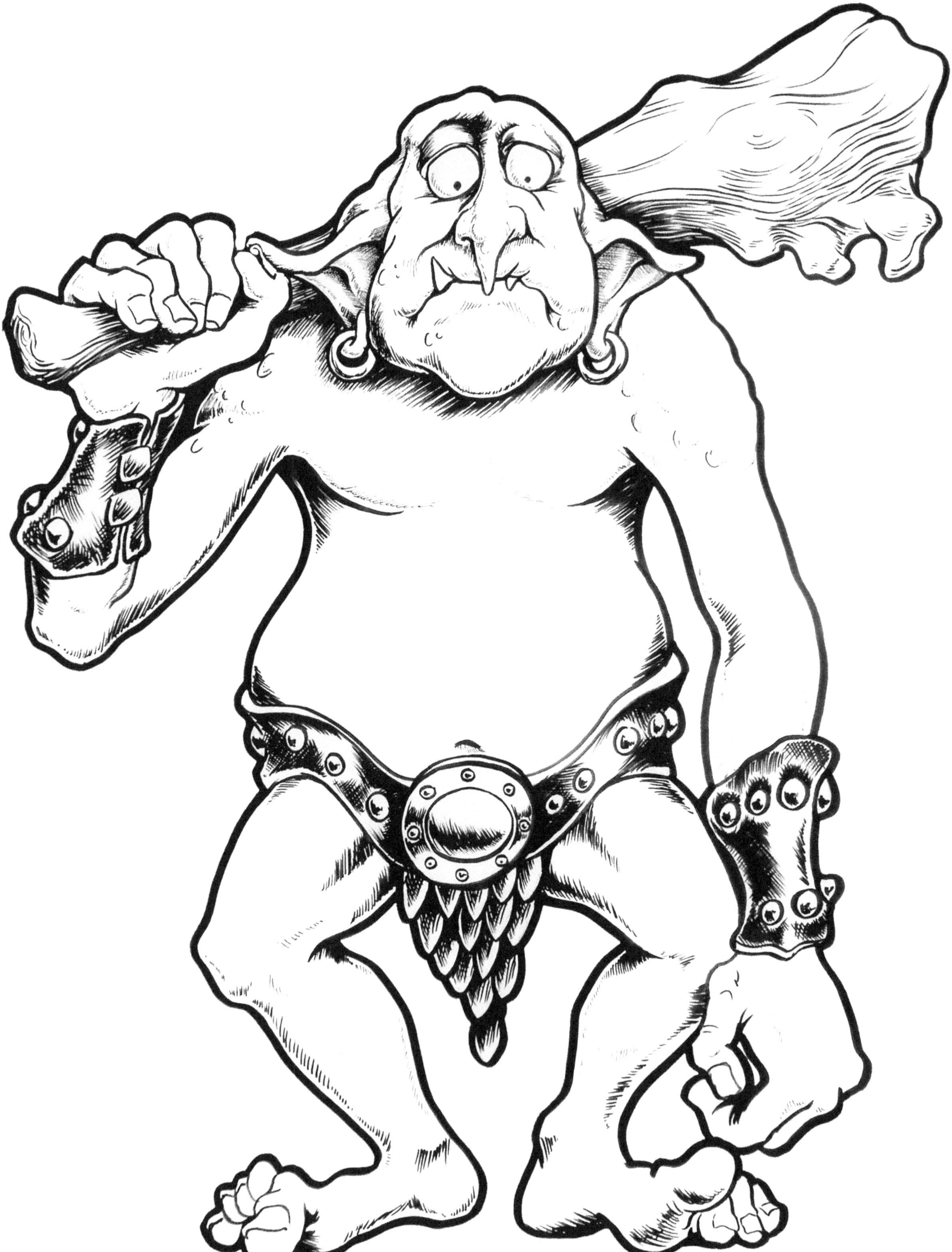

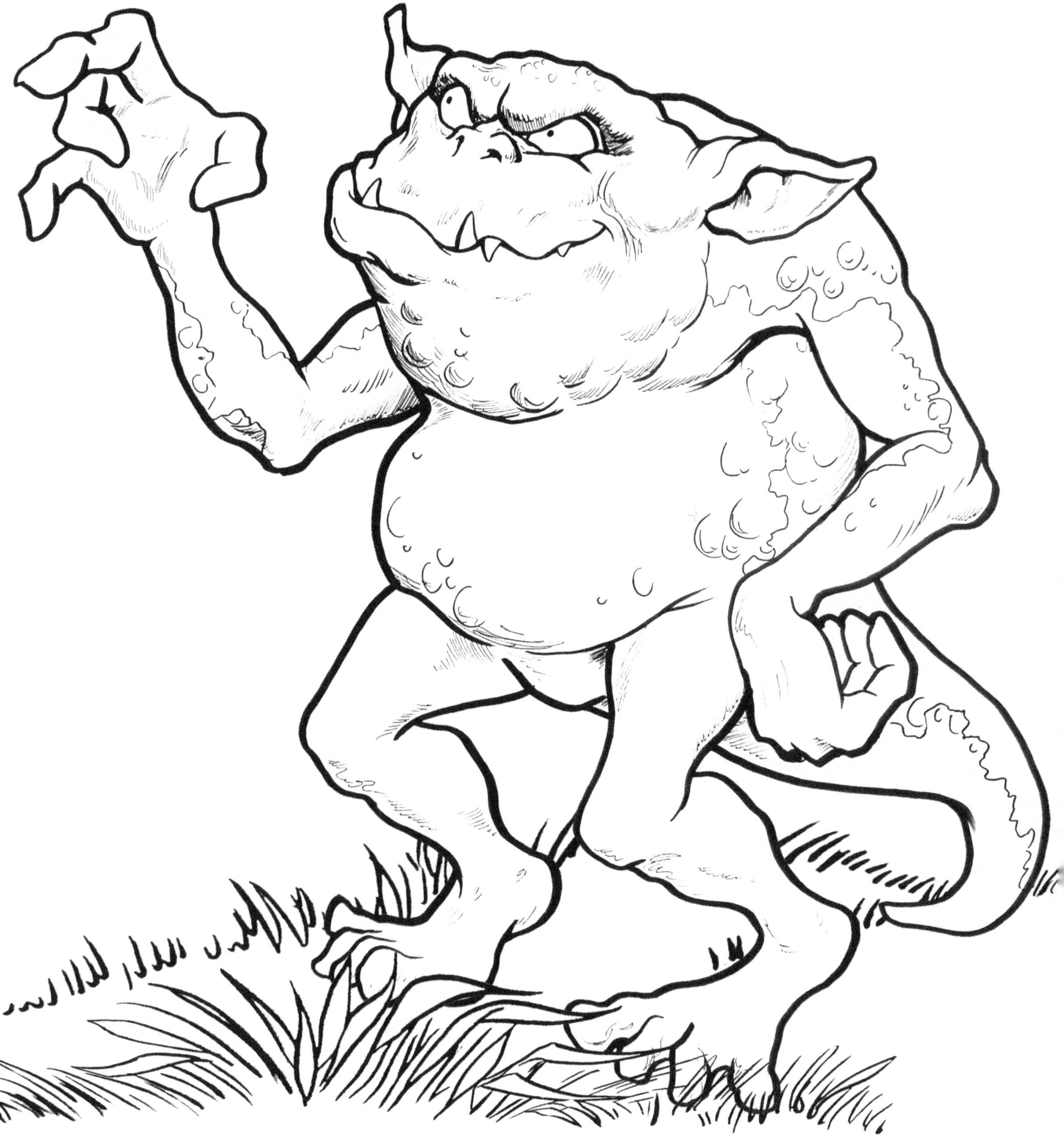

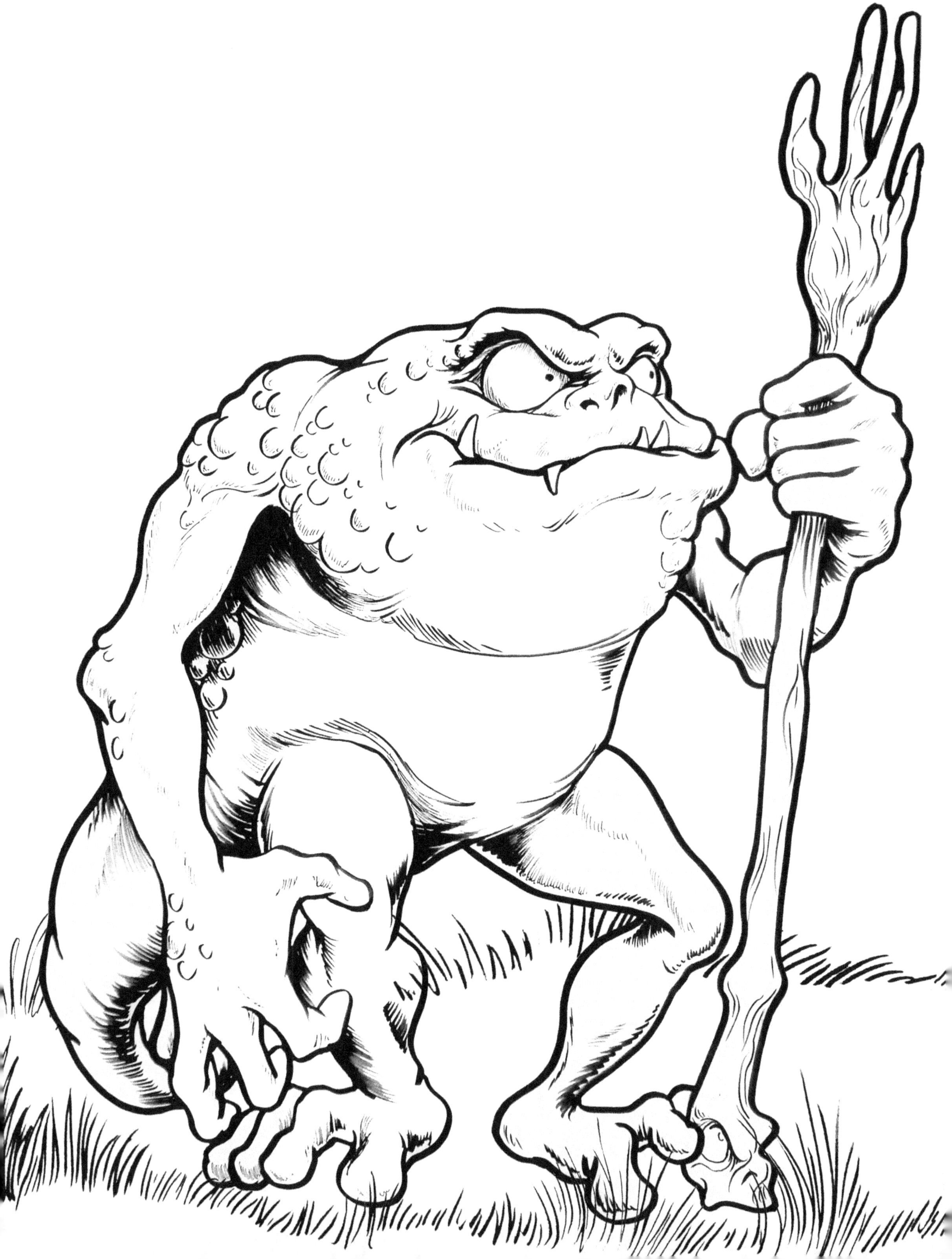

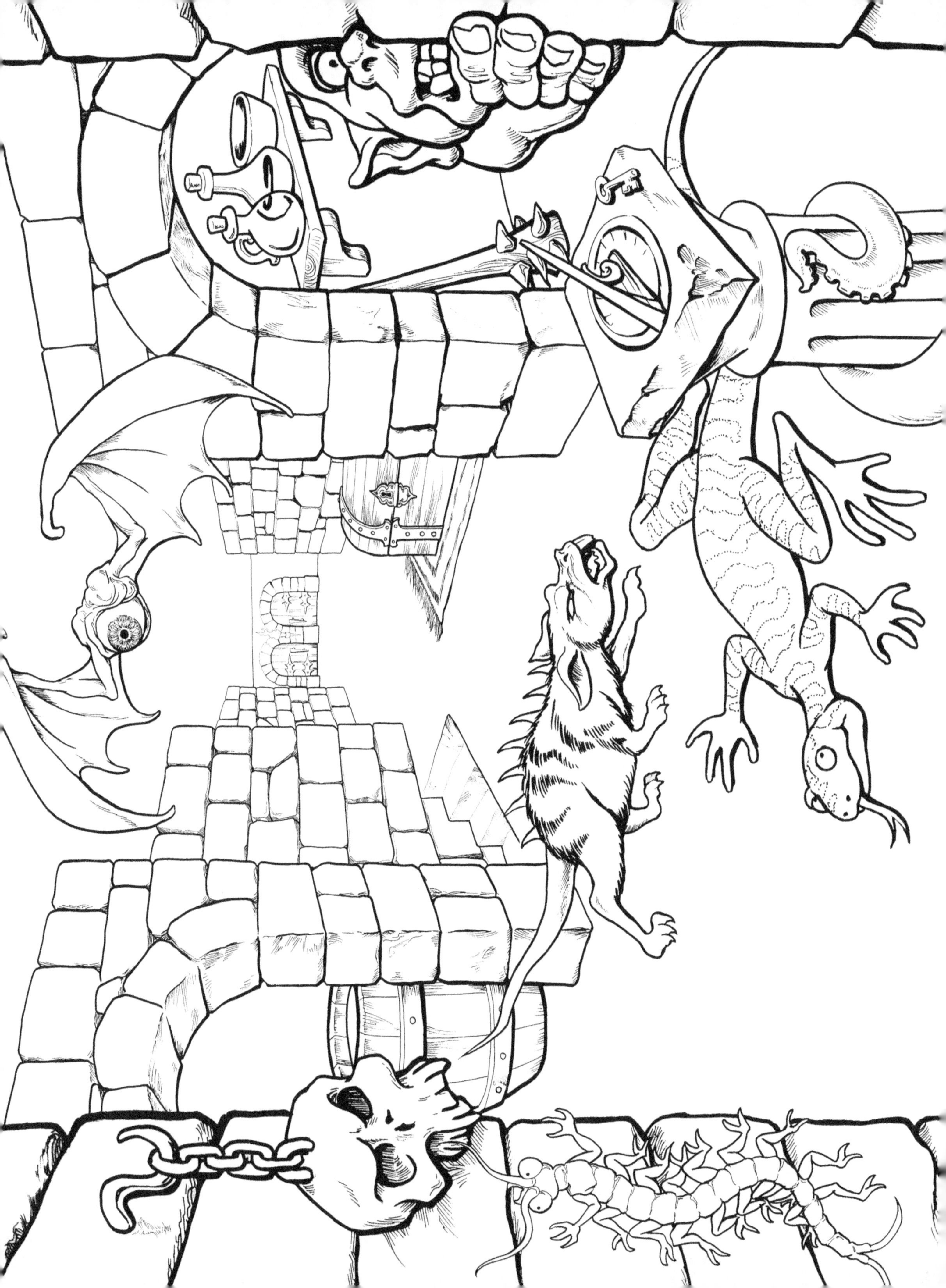

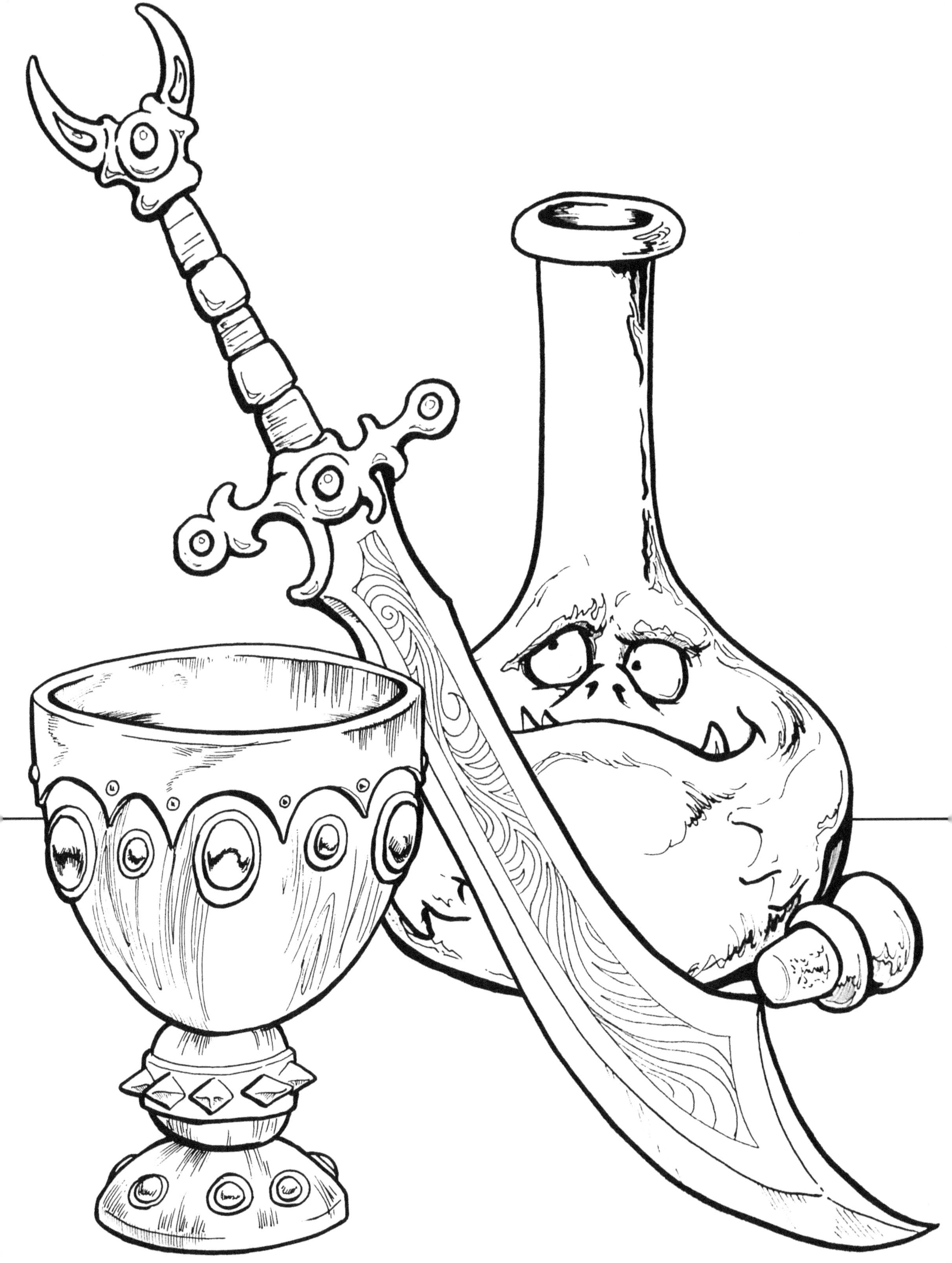

www.ingramcontent.com/pod-product-compliance
Lightning Source LLC
Chambersburg PA
CBHW080612180526
45168CB00007B/2877
* 9 7 8 1 5 1 7 3 0 5 7 2 7 *